School Ties

A Play

George Brockhill

A Samuel French Acting Edition

SAMUEL FRENCH

FOUNDED 1830

SAMUELFRENCH-LONDON.CO.UK
SAMUELFRENCH.COM

CHARACTERS

Derek Ross
Stella, his wife
Brian, their son
Romaine Marsh
Ray
Amy

The action of the play takes place in a detached house in a northern village. It is late evening

Time—the present

SCHOOL TIES

The living-room of a detached house in a northern village

The room is rather bare as some of the furnishings have been taken out pending removal. A door UCR *gives access to the hall and stairs, and a large window* UCL *overlooks the front garden, in which a "For Sale" notice is visible. A door* DL *leads into the lounge, and another door* R *provides entry to the kitchen. The remaining furnishings are of good quality and comprise a small dining table and chairs, easy chair and settee, drinks cabinet and small book-case. Curtains and carpets are as usual. There is a wall-mirror*

Derek Ross, casually dressed, and in his mid-forties, is looking out of the window

Stella, Derek's wife, enters from the kitchen. She is a little younger. She is smartly dressed and attempts a snobbish superiority which she cannot sustain

Stella No-one arrived yet?

Derek No. Probably held up by the fog.

Stella They wouldn't have got a proper look at the house, anyway. It's almost dark. (*She switches on the lights*)

Derek Only time the Marsh woman had, she said. Going up to Scotland on business. And Ray's unlikely to be on time, unless he's changed.

Stella I never thought I'd see Ray and Amy looking for a house.

Derek We don't know that they are yet.

Stella He as good as told us they were. My God! You're not still hoping?

Derek No, I am not.

Stella Not much! You're a married man, with an example to set for a teenage son. He has little respect as it is.

Derek Respect in teenage sons is neither normal nor healthy. Nor is indifference to women in middle-aged men—however ravaged by surgery. But as I'm unlikely to achieve in a brief visit what I failed to achieve over a much longer period five years ago, I can't see what you're getting into a state about.

Stella Well, I hope you won't be quarrelsome if they do turn up.

Derek I shall be quite civil—and ignore him.

Stella We're trying to sell the house—unless you want to give it to her.

Derek We're agreed on the first part. I'd rather not comment on the second. Whatever you may imagine, she was a friend. If you hadn't insisted on us selling the place she might never have turned up at all. I'd forgotten the pair of them.

Brian enters. He is a bright lad, in his middle teens

Brian (*overhearing*) Pair of what, Dad?

Stella Need you ask?

Brian Oh! That pair.

Derek I was talking about Amy and Ray.

Brian I used rather to like Amy. I really did think she was my auntie, you know.

Stella Then you had a very low IQ. I might have known that she'd turn up. If she can't be mistress in one way, she's going to be it in another.

Derek Don't exaggerate.

Brian All's fair in love and war, Mother.

Stella It may be in your school, but it wasn't in mine. We had words like self-respect, and honour.

Brian You can't come the convent stuff, Mother. According to my arithmetic, Dad had to make an honest woman of you.

Stella I was taken advantage of.

Brian It takes two to tango.

Stella Don't just stand there! Hit him!

Derek I will if he uses any more clichés. Anyway, it does, and we did—every Saturday night.

Stella You're worse than he is.

Brian I doubt if we'll get anyone tonight. The fog's thicker than ever.

Stella In that case, I'm going to bed. They can't be serious if they call as late as this. Probably just want to satisfy their curiosity, like the last lot. You never know what you're letting in, or what they're planning to steal. According to *Crimewatch*, there's a clever thief working in the north.

Brian I doubt if you'll get anything pinched, Mother—at your age.

Stella That is neither funny nor original. See that everything's locked up through there, Derek, before you come to bed. Don't forget to check the safe.

Derek I've checked it already. Why don't you lock me up as well!

Stella It could happen. So none of your old Adam.

Brian I've always thought that Adam was unlucky, only having one apple. There's a lot been done for consumer choice since then.

Stella And when you can get a Golden Delicious, why bother with a sour old cooker like me?

Brian That's rampant jealousy, Mother!

Derek This conversation is becoming tedious. At least I shan't have to endure Ray.

Brian goes to close the curtains

I'm not in the mood for a lot of damned silly questions.

Brian (*looking out*) Hey! Someone's turning in—a woman. It must be Mrs Marsh.

Stella Oh, damn! At bedtime. (*She joins Brian at the window*) Now where . . .?

Derek Something troubling you, Stella?

Stella Something—at the back of my mind.

Brian You should have it seen to.

Stella That walk. No. Maybe I'm tired.

Brian Nicely built. Good thatch, too.

Derek If it is her, you'd better hang on for a few minutes.

Stella Get her to come back tomorrow, if you can. I'd prefer to look her over in daylight.

The doorbell rings

Derek I'll ask her for a surveyor's report.

Derek exits

Stella Is your room tidy, Brian? I've had enough snooty remarks.

Brian You've made a few, as well.

There are voices off and Derek reappears followed by Mrs Marsh. Romaine Marsh is about Stella's age, but there the resemblance ends. Her colouring is in contrast to Stella's, and she is abrupt, and down-to-earth in manner. Her clothes are simple, but, judging by her raincoat and handbag, of good quality

Romaine It's kind of you to receive me at this time of night. I am
most dreadfully late.
Derek You did well to get here at all with the weather as it is. My
wife, Stella, and Brian, my son.

They exchange greetings

Let me take your coat.
Romaine Thank you! It is a bit damp

She removes her coat and Derek takes it into the hall

I won't stay longer than is necessary.
Brian How far have you walked?
Romaine I pulled in at the *Star and Garter*, down the road.
Couldn't face the fog any more. I was beginning to see things
which weren't there.
Stella Where did you say you came from?
Romaine What? Ah! On the phone. Reading. Not my home town.
I was brought up in Sheffield.
Derek So was Stella.
Romaine Really?
Derek Oh, yes. Take a seat.
Romaine (*sitting down*) Thank you! Well! They do say that the
world is getting smaller. Whereabouts were you?
Stella East side. Off Norfolk Road. A new residential quarter it
was then. I don't suppose you'd know it.
Romaine I knew it well.
Brian The world is shrinking by the minute.
Romaine Yes. We lived just a few streets away. Glencoe Road.
Stella (*staring at Romaine*) Were you ever at Westleigh High?
Romaine Yes. Were you?
Stella Yes. Who was the Head—Miss Jollingham?
Romaine That's right. You—you're not—Stella Hindle?
Stella I am. And you're—Romy Padgett?
Romaine Yes. Well, blow me down!
Derek I've a feeling that this is going to be a long night. Have you
had anything to eat?
Romaine At the *Star and Garter*, thanks!
Derek But you won't say no to a drink.
Stella She's changed if she does.
Romaine No tales, Stella. Remember—glass houses, and all that.

Brian I'm beginning to think that there should be a government health warning attached to marriage certificates: "This document can seriously damage your memory".

Romaine Nice sense of humour, this boy. Surprising, really.

Stella What's surprising about it?

Romaine Well—as I recollect, you were polished rather than bright.

Stella If your memory wasn't plainly failing, I'd say you were insufferable.

One is trying to hold on to the veil over her past, the other maliciously trying to lift it

Romaine Oh, come on! You can't have forgotten those exam results.

Derek If you can tear yourselves away from the Quadrangle for a few minutes, girls, we'll have a drink. Mrs Marsh?

Romaine A small gin and tonic, please. And the name's Romaine.

Derek Right! Bacardi for you, Stella. Brian doesn't—as yet.

Romaine Wise boy. Do you remember how ill we were, Stella, that first time? Ah! It all comes back now.

Derek It apparently did then.

Brian I think you should have put me to bed early, Mother.

Romaine We were very young, and perhaps I exaggerate.

Stella You don't exaggerate. You invent.

Romaine Great days, nevertheless. Cheers! Those boys at the Army Camp. What was the name of yours—Alan Something-or-other?

Derek Er—wasn't there something about selling a house?

Romaine Oh, of course. All these reminiscences. I do run on.

Stella Yes. Let's get down to business—then you can run off.

Derek You won't be able to see much of the outside.

Romaine That doesn't matter. Got a photograph from the Agent. Large area of garden—that's what tempted me. Space for the dogs.

Stella Dogs?

Romaine I breed 'em. Kennels, you know. Don't mind paying over the odds if it's suitable.

Stella I don't fancy having my house over-run by dogs. I see enough of them on the pavements. Dirty things.

Brian Don't put your foot in it, Mother!

Romaine Just want to check on the general layout of the house. I like convenience.

Brian We have two of those.

Derek Don't be an ass, Brian! It's pretty basic, really. (*He crosses to the lounge door*) 'Fraid the lounge is in a bit of a mess. Stella's already packing.

Stella Our new house is almost ready.

Romaine Really! (*She looks at Derek*) Good at backing winners, Stella. Always was—on and off the course.

Brian glances enquiringly at Stella. Romaine peers into the room

Seems satisfactory. I should be able to make something out of that.

Stella Yes. It'll look well with metal doors and wire.

Derek You'll want to see the bedrooms, of course.

Stella Not with you she won't. I'll show her up.

Romaine I've no doubt that you'll try.

Stella What is that obscene perfume you're wearing?

Romaine I don't know. I got it from the Vet's to bring the bitches on heat.

Stella and Romaine exit

Brian Why am I thinking about St Trinians?

Derek (*laughing*) A chummy pair, aren't they.

Brian There's a few questions I'd like to ask Mother.

Derek Better to let sleeping dogs lie.

There is the sound of a car

Brian There's a car pulling in. Could it be the others?

Derek It could.

Car door slams. Derek moves uneasily

Brian You look like a man who's about to be kicked in a tender place.

There is a knock at the front door

A moment later Ray enters the room. He is a biggish man, well-dressed, self-important, a pipe-smoker and generally rather irritating. He is followed by Amy who is Ray's opposite—petite and serious and unassumingly dressed

Ray Sorry we're late, old man. Devil of a night!

Derek We didn't think you'd brave the fog.

Ray Rather wish we hadn't. Damned car! Limping along on two cylinders. Lucky to get here at all. (*He turns to Amy*) You remember the little woman? (*He smirks*) Of course you do.

Derek's look is a mute epithet but he greets Amy cordially

Derek You look well. I didn't expect you two to be house-hunting.

Amy It—came on rather suddenly.

Ray Not the way you're thinking, old boy.

Derek I wasn't thinking anything.

Ray I managed to persuade her without that.

Amy I'm beginning to wish you hadn't.

Ray Can't back out, now we've found a house. We're committed—for trial, eh? (*He laughs*) Sorry, old man! You can't win 'em all.

Derek Neither can you. I think you've been forestalled.

Ray Ah! I wondered about the glasses. I suppose you couldn't . . .? Amy's got cold feet. No fun whichever way you look at it.

Derek You'll get a bloody cold shoulder, if you talk like that. What do you want?

Ray Scotch. Neat and large. And a hair of the same dog for Amy.

Amy A small one, please.

Derek pours the drinks

It's a nice house.

Ray Yes. Who's beaten me to it?

Derek (*handing drinks*) Old aquaintance of Stella's.

Ray Really?

Derek Yes. Someone who breeds dogs.

Ray H'm! Mind you don't get bitten, old man.

Stella and Romaine enter from the stairs. Ray greets Stella effusively

Well, Stella! Nice to see you again. (*He kisses her on the cheek*) You're looking in good shape—as ever. Young Brian's growing, too. More like his father than you.

Stella (*sweetly*) Yes. He's almost a man.

Derek reacts

Brian (*glancing at Amy*) "Whom the gods wish to destroy . . .!"
Ray (*to Romaine*) So you're the lady who beat me at the last fence.
Romaine I'd a head start.
Derek You can say that again.
Romaine Name's Marsh. Romaine. Stella and I are old friends.
Stella We were at school together.
Ray Old friends, eh.
Stella I said we were at school together.
Ray No go, Amy. Old girl network. School ties and all that.
    We've no chance. Got to fix the car, anyway. Clear field, old
    boy. Take your pick. Sorry, Stella! Just my little joke.
Stella You must explain it to me sometime.
Ray Don't mind if I borrow your garage for half-an-hour, do you
    old man? And a tool-kit, if you've got one.
Derek Open the garage doors, Brian. He'll find all he needs on the
    bench.
Ray I'll have to run your car out.
Derek It's gone for MOT.
Ray Good! I'll call you if we need a push.

   Ray and Brian exit

Amy (*laughing*) When Ray wants anything, he believes in asking
    for it.
Derek (*disgruntled*) He's certainly asking for it now.
Stella You couldn't very well refuse to help them. They'll want to
    get home.
Amy We shan't go home to-night. We're hoping to find a hotel.
Stella (*superior*) It seems to be the usual thing to do. Whichever
    finger the ring is on.

Romaine laughs

   What's the matter with you?
Romaine Nothing. Just thinking.
Stella Well, don't.
Amy I think I'd like to go upstairs, if you don't mind.
Derek Of course, Amy. It's second door on the right.

   Amy exits

Romaine Going over the top a bit, aren't you?

Stella (*glancing at Derek*) She's a scalp-collector.
Romaine Ah! Well, one must collect something. *Chaçun à son goût.* You had a penchant for jewellery, I believe. You must have quite a little pile by now.

Stella glares

Derek (*grimly*) She has.
Romaine Diamonds are a girl's best friend, eh?
Derek When they're real. Stella can't always tell the difference.
Stella That's a lie!
Derek I don't think we should talk about it.
Romaine Quite right. A careless word, and half the criminal fraternity in the district can be alerted. If it's valuable, put it in the bank.
Stella I can't go to the bank every time I have an evening out.
Derek Why not? I have to.
Stella Don't be so stingy!
Romaine This friend of yours, Ray. Can you trust him?
Derek I thought I could, until he deprived me of a beautiful friendship five years ago.
Romaine Amy?
Stella Things that are lying about get picked up.
Romaine So it was your scalp. I can understand the soreness. Didn't expect it to last this long, eh?
Stella It should never have been started.
Romaine Human frailty, Stella. Nobody's immune. Remember that trainee teacher at West—?
Stella (*annoyed*) All right! Don't keep raking things up. School-days are over—forgotten.
Romaine Not true. We always carry the torch.
Stella Very well! Carry the damned thing, but don't try to burn me with it.
Romaine Only urging caution. While you're watching the front door, thieves can be busy at the back.
Stella Or upstairs. I'd better go.

She hurries out

Derek (*calling*) Don't be silly! She's obsessed!
Romaine Yes. Rather barking up the wrong tree there. Of course, someone could be using her.

Derek Don't remind me.

Romaine I don't mean in that way. But many a dove has been turned into a stool-pigeon. Stella's nervy.

Derek She's no need to be—on either count, now.

Romaine Don't like Ray much, do you?

Derek No—blast him!

Romaine It often happens. The nicest girls get the biggest rogues. Assuming that he is, of course. In any case I can't see anyone risking imprisonment for what Stella has.

Derek I'm with you there.

Romaine Mind you she does talk—always did. When we were at school you'd have thought she had the crown jewels. Rings, pins—a necklace worth thousands. (*She pauses*) Nobody believed her. That was Stella. She always had to be top dog.

Brian enters

Derek Trouble?

Brian (*uncertainly*) N . . . no. We got it into the garage all right—with a lot of exertion.

Derek It wouldn't start?

Brian Not a spark.

Derek Does he know what the problem is?

Brian I'm not sure that there is one.

Derek There must be if it won't start.

Brian You'd think so. Only—he threw his coat on the bench, and when I reached over to get him a spanner, I put my hand on it. There was something hard in the pocket. I could almost swear that it was the rotary arm off the distributor.

Derek Are you telling me that the breakdown is a fake?

Brian I suppose it could have been a spare, but it's a funny place to carry it.

Derek glances at Romaine. Her expression feeds his speculation

Amy enters

Amy Have you and Stella had a row?

Derek Not more than usual. Why?

Amy When I passed her door she seemed to be frantically packing everything she could lay her hands on.

Derek Bit of a trauma, moving house.

Romaine Perhaps she's afraid of losing something.

Ray enters. His coat is wet, and he looks annoyed

Ray I don't know what's wrong with the damned thing. It looks like a garage job.
Amy Is it raining?
Ray Like the devil. As if the fog weren't enough.
Romaine Oh, dear!
Brian The weathermen got it right.
Ray Is there a local garage?
Derek Not at this time of night.
Ray Looks like we'll have to wait until morning. Sorry, old girl!
Derek There'll be all-night garages nearer Leeds. You could telephone.
Ray I'd have to pay through the nose, even if they could find the place. I'd rather stay put. And I'd like to go upstairs a minute, and get rid of this grime.
Derek You can do that in the kitchen sink.
Ray I rather wanted to get rid of something else as well.
Derek Forget about the kitchen sink.
Ray Oh! And can I have a clean towel? Bit prone to dermititis.
Derek With a skin like yours? Ask Stella. She's up there. And don't surprise her. She can be dangerous.
Ray I'll cough.

Ray exits

Derek What's a nice girl like you doing with an oaf like that?
Amy He's better when you get to know him.
Derek (*with a despairing gesture*) It's beyond me!
Romaine He looked pretty wet.
Derek He always does.
Brian (*looking out*) We can't send Mrs Marsh out in this, Dad. It's pouring down.
Amy Lucky for us we've got the car, immobile though it is.
Derek Are you going to sleep out there?
Amy Well—yes, if Ray insists.
Derek Over my dead body!
Brian That'll be colder still.

Stella enters

Derek All right?

Stella No. Ray's wiping his grubby hands on one of my best towels. He's no respecter of property.

Brian He must be a developer.

Derek He's a bloody late one. We can't let Romaine walk back to the pub in this, Stella. She'll be soaked to the skin.

Stella Nobody but a fool would have left the car behind.

Brian It isn't as if you're strangers, Mother.

Stella No. I'd be happier if we were.

Romaine Thank you, Stella! If it's any trouble, I don't mind walking ...

Stella No. You can stay. At least you'll see a little more of the house.

Ray enters. He takes out his pipe, and puts his tobacco-pouch on the table

I hope you aren't going to smoke.

Ray Oh! Er—no. Sorry old girl! I'm rather a sucker for the pipe. (*He puts the empty pipe in his mouth*)

Brian Look! If Mrs Marsh shares your room, Mother, I can go in with Dad, and Amy and Ray can have the spare double.

Ray Good thinking, boy. How about it, old girl?

Amy Not tonight, Napoleon!

Ray H'm! A pity. Looks like I'll have to kip down here on the settee.

Stella (*dubiously*) I don't like it.

Ray Neither does Amy, it would appear, or I wouldn't be on the settee.

Stella Don't be coarse!

Brian Shall Dad and I take the double, then Amy can have my single?

Stella Why are you so concerned?

Brian It's interesting. Like one of those maze problems. How does A get to B without having to pass C?

Amy I find this rather embarrassing.

Derek I agree—not to mention idiotic.

Romaine I think we should all do as Brian suggests. You won't get a better arrangement. We shall all rise in the morning without a stain on our characters. Come along, Stella! Let's go up. Gosh! I find this quite exciting. Reminds me of old times in the dorm. Remember the pillow-fights we used to have?

Stella If you're going to be childish, you'll go out in the rain.
Romaine Only natural you should want to forget. You always got the worst of it.
Stella I did not! You're the one who's forgetting.

Stella and Romaine move towards the stairs

Derek How about the pub, Romaine? If they're expecting you back——.
Romaine I am forgetting. May I use your phone?
Derek In the hall.

Romaine goes out.

Ray moves up to the hall doorway

Going out?
Ray Just wondering about the garage. Shall I lock it?
Derek You do it, Brian.
Stella And make sure that everything else is locked as well.

Stella goes upstairs

Derek We will. (*He takes keys from his pocket and locks the lounge door*)
Ray A cautious woman, Stella.

Derek smiles

Derek You'll have coffee and sandwiches?
Amy Just coffee for me, Derek, thanks.
Ray She's a weight-watcher, old man.
Derek She doesn't seem to have much option with you around.
Ray Naughty! Naughty!

Derek goes into the kitchen

Brian goes out to the garage

Amy (*in an undertone*) No safe upstairs. I think it must be through there.
Ray I'm pretty sure it is. Could be tricky. There's french windows opening onto the lawn. I'll have a reccy when they've gone to bed.
Amy Sh!

Derek enters with coffee and sandwiches

Derek Still hot from the pot, and fresh from the fridge.

Romaine appears in the doorway

All right?
Romaine Yes, thanks! They're even giving a reduction. Good-
night!

Romaine goes upstairs

Derek puts down the tray

Derek Where have you been since I last saw you?
Ray Here and there.
Derek Doing what?
Ray This and that.
Derek Why did I ask?
Ray You tell me, old man.
Derek Will you be going back tomorrow?
Ray It depends—on Mrs Marsh.
Derek Oh, yes. The house.
Amy Has she said anything?
Derek Not to me.
Ray They're probably bargaining upstairs.
Derek Then it's likely to be a pretty hard bargain.
Amy (*smiling*) This conversation is becoming too esoteric for me.
I'm going to bed.
Derek You haven't finished your coffee.
Amy I won't drink any more, if you don't mind. It's a long way to
the end of the corridor.
Ray It's the A to B stuff. Don't want any misunderstandings, do
we?
Derek (*sourly to Amy*) Better lock your door as well.
Amy Not necessary with your wife around. She'll probably lock
yours.

Derek growls

But I'll lock my chastity belt just in case. See you in the morning.

Amy goes out and upstairs

Derek Good-night, Amy! You've got a gem there. Lucky devil!
Ray A very collectable little item, old man.

Brian enters

Derek Better let me have the keys, Brian. You go to bed. I'll be up in a minute.
Brian Yes. OK.

Brian exits

Derek Make yourself comfortable, Ray—if you can.
Ray Don't worry about me, old man. I'll be as right as rain.
Derek That's what I thought when I looked outside.

Derek goes upstairs

Ray (*smiling*) Right as rain, old man. (*He takes off his shoes and switches off the main lights and table-lamp. Taking a small torch from his pocket, he goes to the hall door and listens. Satisfied, he crosses to the lounge door, produces a small bunch of keys, tries first one and then another*) You've a lot to learn, Derek. (*He opens the door and briefly scans the room*) Ah, yes! (*He closes the door quietly, leaving it unlocked, switches off the torch and settles down on the settee*) Now! We wait.

The semi-darkness dims into a blackout, followed by the slow bringing up of bluish moonlight to denote the passing of time. A clock strikes two. Ray gets up quietly, pulls aside one half of the curtains, and looks out

Fine! Just fine. (*He goes to the lounge door and opens it. The catch clicks*) Damn! (*He goes in*)

Derek and Brian appear in the hall doorway, shadowy figures in pyjamas

Derek (*whispering*) You were right. He isn't here.
Brian I told you. I heard him moving about.
Derek Sh! (*He looks towards the lounge door*) Now how the devil did he get in there?
Brian Must have picked the lock. What are we going to do?
Derek Make a citizen's arrest.
Brian Shouldn't we call the police?
Derek They'll take ages. He'll be gone by then. Besides—we've got to think about Amy.
Brian You have.

Derek Shut up! Let me deal with him.
Brian He's bigger than you are.
Derek Yes. But I've worn the black belt.
Brian Only to keep your trousers up.
Derek Don't argue! I'll go round to the french windows, and tackle him from that side. You get behind that door. Here! Take this. (*He picks up a large ornamental jar*) If there's any doubt, hit him—hard. I won't be long so don't make a sound.

Derek goes out quietly

Brian stealthily takes up his position behind the door. There is a brief silence, then a muffled exclamation of pain off L

Derek backs out through the door dragging Ray

Brian, unable to see clearly, and having prejudged the contest in any case, steps out and brings the jar down on Derek's head. Derek goes down amid fragments of pottery. Brian crosses quickly and switches on the lights

Ray (*struggling up*) That was a damned unfilial thing to do. (*His voice is sharper, more commanding*)
Brian I—I thought it was you.
Ray Thanks! Your father banged my head on the safe, and you were going to finish me off.

Derek groans and sits up, holding his head

Derek Oooooh! Who the blazes did that?
Brian Are you hurt, Dad?
Derek What the hell do you think?
Brian You did tell me to hit him.
Derek I didn't tell you to hit me.
Brian I couldn't see. And I certainly couldn't see how you could win. You surprise me.
Ray I was surprised as well, when I found myself head-butting a metal safe. You'll have some explaining to do about that.
Derek I'll have some explaining to do!
Ray That's what I said.
Derek I don't think the blood is getting to my head.
Ray (*dabbing his forehead with a handkerchief*) I wish I could say

the same. (*He goes to the table and pours out two drinks*) Here! Drink this—and get up.

Derek (*struggling to his feet*) You've got a bloody nerve! You rob my safe, make free with my whisky, and then order me about in my own house. Well, you won't get away with it. I've got the evidence, and I've got the witnesses, and——

Brian Hang on a minute! There's something I don't understand.

Derek You will when his case comes up. It's my guess that——

Ray (*curtly*) Shut up, and let the boy speak.

Derek Well, I'm damned!

Brian Calm down, Dad! Can't you see? He—he's not himself.

Derek He's no worse than I am, so don't make excuses for him. He's a crook, relying on a decent woman to give him respectability.

Ray If you think that, you're concussed.

Brian His voice has changed. Haven't you noticed?

Derek Then he's going to have a very short manhood, because it'll have changed again before I've finished with him. Ring the police.

Ray I know there are mitigating circumstances, but you can get into serious trouble making threats against the police—to the police.

Derek Making threats against the police? To—to what?

Ray shows his ID card

Brian I did try to warn you. If he'd been a crook, he'd have scarpered when I knocked you out.

Derek I will have that whisky. I don't feel well.

Ray There's nothing wrong with you that a word from Amy won't put right.

Derek Are you saying that—she isn't——?

Ray She isn't.

Derek And Stella's necklace was never in danger?

Ray I didn't say that. It was, and is yet. You've been looking in the wrong direction.

Derek You surely don't mean Romaine?

Ray She's a clever lady.

Derek But she and Stella were at school together.

Ray Who pointed the finger of suspicion at me?

Brian Well—I suppose I did—at first. And then——

Ray Mrs Marsh? I think your safe is still open, Derek.

Derek I'd forgotten about that. Go and lock it, Brian. And the french windows.

Brain exits L

What exactly were you doing in there?

Ray Checking the value of the stakes. That's quite an exquisite little necklace that Stella has. Don't often see them as fine as that. Any idea of it's worth?

Derek Not really—no. Family things are over-prized, and over-valued. Could be worth a bit.

Ray I'd take it to Sotheby's.

Derek Good God! Is it in that class?

Ray Experts like Mrs Marsh don't work for nothing. Damn it! I'd have had her if you'd kept your nose out.

Derek I'd the same feeling five years ago, when you went off with Amy.

Ray I'd have caught her on the job.

Derek frowns

I mean Mrs Marsh, fathead! Nobody's going to steal anything now, after the row we've made.

Brian enters in alarm

Brian Dad! It's gone.

Derek What's gone?

Brian Mother's necklace. The rest of the stuff's there, but the necklace isn't.

Derek Are you sure?

Brian Of course I'm sure. I locked the french windows first, and then went over to the safe. There's no necklace. See for yourselves.

Derek and Ray hurry out in disbelief, and quickly return

Ray Well! Well!

Derek Yes. Well—well. You were the last in that room, Ray. Are you really a policeman? Anyone can fake an ID card.

Ray It isn't faked, and I wasn't the last one in there. (*He looks at Brian*)

Derek Now you're being bloody absurd!

Ray And so are you. If you've any doubt you can ring the station on my car-phone. Come on!
Derek Where are we going?
Ray To catch her, of course.
Derek At the pub?
Ray Her car isn't at the pub.
Derek She rang them.
Ray She pretended to ring. I was listening. Ten to one her car is somewhere much nearer. We've no time to argue. Get your coat.

They move towards the hall doorway

> *Romaine walks calmly in from the stairs. She is wearing a dressing gown over other borrowed night attire*

There is silence as Derek and Brian look enquiringly at Ray

Romaine What's all the noise about? We thought the house was being burgled. Stella's getting quite cross.
Derek I think you'd better ask Stella to come down.
Romaine (*shrugging*) On your head be it.

> *She goes upstairs*

Derek I wish she hadn't said that. What the hell am I going to tell Stella?
Brian Better tell her the truth, Dad.
Derek I don't know what the bloody truth is.
Brian She'll probably agree with you.
Derek Over to you, defective Inspector.
Ray (*annoyed*) Cut the sarcasm! You aren't in the clear yet—any of you.

> *Romaine enters*

Romaine I get this feeling of unreality. Am I really facing two bruised and bleeding angry men, with only someone else's night attire between me and dishonour?
Ray Very amusing, madam! But you'll have to do better than that.

Stella enters. She also is in nightdress and dressing-gown, but she is dishevelled and her hair is covered in down and feathers. The three men stare at her

Derek I think she has.
Brian Mother! Have you gone into the moult or something?

Romaine is shaking with laughter

Stella What?
Brian Your hair.
Stella (*going to the mirror, then turning on Romaine*) You fool!
Romaine You threw down the gauntlet. Here! Take my comb—
    and don't be such a goose.
Stella I'll kill her! (*She tidies her hair*)
Derek That's rather knocked the stuffing out of the case, Ray.
Ray Not out of mine.
Stella What's he talking about?
Derek Your necklace has disappeared.
Stella Disappeared?
Ray I think it's been stolen.
Stella Oh, my God! When?
Derek Only a short time ago.
Romaine You see, Stella.
Stella Haven't you phoned the police?
Brian They're here.
Stella I'd a premonition that those two were up to no good. How
    do you mean, they're here?
Derek Ray's a detective.
Stella You believe that?
Derek There's no denying it, I'm afraid.

Ray produces the ID card

Stella (*nonplussed*) I'm having a nightmare. Detective Inspector?
Romaine (*dismayed*) How—how did they get in?
Ray They already were in.
Romaine Hiding?
Ray Masquerading.
Romaine (*recovering*) You seem to be quite an authority on that. I
    don't see how anyone could—— I mean, we were all here.
Stella We were not, Romaine. There was one up—— (*She
    realises, and turns on Derek*) I knew you'd carry that bondage
    fantasy too far.
Romaine I think we're going to be asked some embarrassing
    questions. Are we all under suspicion. Inspector?

Ray Not all, Mrs Marsh.

Stella I don't see how anyone could steal it. Everything was locked up.

Derek Yes. Well—there was a misunderstanding.

Brian It was dark, and we—mistook each other for burglars.

Stella You need your heads looking at!

Romaine (*looking intently at Stella*) Rather reminds me of school, when Rita's gold watch went missing.

Derek At school?

Romaine Yes. Some of them thought we'd taken it. Quite wrongly, of course. It turned up in one of the teacher's pockets, and he swore he didn't know it was there. A likely story. Remember, Stella?

Stella (*thoughtfully*) Yes, I do.

Ray I'd rather we stuck to the present, if you don't mind.

Amy enters. She is fully dressed

Stella Haven't you forgotten your helmet and boots?

Amy Ah! So the cat's out of the bag.

Ray And more importantly, the necklace is out of the safe.

Amy Stolen?

Ray Yes.

Amy (*looking at Ray's blood-stained forehead and the shattered jar*) Robbery with violence. Someone from outside?

Ray No. Robbery and violence. And some damned fool from inside.

Amy I don't understand.

Ray Just as well. I'd rather you didn't.

Amy What are you going to do?

Ray Have the lot of them searched, starting with Mrs Marsh.

Romaine (*sitting down and bursting into tears*) I didn't do it. Stella and I have always been friends. Loyal friends.

Ray We shall see. Take her upstairs Amy, and search her.

Brian Aren't you supposed to caution them or something? Anything that's taken down——

Romaine (*howling*) I don't want anything taken down.

Stella Oh, for goodness sake, stop crying. Haven't you got a handkerchief?

Romaine (*snivelling*) Yes—somewhere. (*She fumbles in her pocket, extracts a rather large handkerchief and starts to wipe her eyes*)

Stella Here! Let me. You're wiping make-up all over your face. (*She takes the handkerchief and applies it gently to Romaine's face*) Now, shut up, and do as the Inspector asks. There's nothing to be afraid of. (*She puts the handkerchief in her pocket*)
Romaine Thank you, Stella! You always were a comfort in trouble. (*Crying again*) To be treated like a common criminal!
Ray Get on with it, Amy.
Romaine (*rising*) It's so humiliating. I haven't got a thing.
Ray This is a search, madam, not a medical examination.
Derek Here! Steady on.
Ray She's tried the injured innocence lark before, but it isn't going to work this time.

Amy and Romaine exit

Stella Well! Injured innocence or not, we'd better clear this lot up, or there'll be some injured feet. (*She begins picking up pieces of the broken jar*) I thought I saw some bits over there in the corner, Ray. Can you—detect anything?

Ray scrutinises the area indicated. Stella moves Ray's tobacco-pouch and places a little pile of fragments on the table

Derek I'll get the dust-pan.

He goes into the kitchen

Stella remains at the table. Ray and Brian are still looking for splinters

Ray I can't see anything here.

Derek comes back with the dust-pan

Stella I must have been mistaken.

Derek puts the pieces in the dust-pan

Derek Take these out, Brian.

Brian takes the pan and goes out through the kitchen

I think you're taking this remarkably well, Stella. That necklace is valuable.
Stella I'm sure that the Inspector is doing all he can. I've no doubt that he'll find it in time.

Ray Thanks for the vote of confidence, Stella. I'm only sorry that a friend of yours should be involved.

Stella There's no need to be. It's no deep friendship, I assure you.

She goes to the mirror again, and turning her head from one side to the other, removes a remaining feather

Ray Good!

Amy enters with Romaine

Well?

Amy Nothing.

Ray (*disbelieving*) You mean that she's clean?

Romaine Of course, Inspector. Couldn't you smell the soap? I think you owe me an apology.

Ray You will receive your dues.

Romaine You're a hard man to convince. How could I steal anything if you were in there safeguarding—the safe. Prior to that, I was with Stella.

Brian enters

Stella If they'd left the safe as it was this would never have happened. Trust the men to make a mess of things.

Brian Couldn't we simply admit that it's been stolen, and collect the insurance money?

Ray I don't think that would be honest, at this stage.

Brian It would be better than the lies that have been told about how it came into the family.

Derek Shut up, Brian! You're making things worse.

Ray He certainly isn't making them any better—nor are the rest of you. Have you any objection to being searched, Stella?

Stella Me! You think I'd steal my own necklace?

Ray People sometimes have things planted on them.

Stella Yes. Like skin and hair, if I lose my temper.

Romaine Oh, go on, Stella. Just to please the Inspector. I rather enjoyed it—and it'll make Amy's day.

Stella glares

Ray Sorry! I do have my job to do.

Stella Very well!

Ray It's only your clothing we're interested in.

Stella Thank you very much! I'll see you on the catwalk.

She goes angrily upstairs, followed by Amy

Romaine Easily upset, Stella.
Derek Yes. Will Amy be able to cope?
Ray I think so. She has a very effective arm-lock.

Romaine laughs, and strolls over to the window

Romaine (*looking out*) It's a beautifully clear night, now. I could
  get to Scotland by daylight.
Ray No one leaves until this thing is found.
Romaine Well, can I get dressed? I'm rather cold.
Ray No. Well, all right. But just a minute. (*He goes to the bottom
  of the stairs and calls*) Amy!

There is an indistinct reply

When you've finished with Stella, Mrs Marsh is coming up to
get dressed. See that there's no funny business.

Amy replies indistinctly

You can go on up.
Romaine Thank you, Inspector!

She goes out

Ray (*sitting down*) Something's gone wrong. I don't know how,
  but it has. She was in there.
Brian I didn't smell any perfume. Surely with that——
Ray She's wearing your mother's clothes.
Brian I can't credit it. She seems such a jolly woman.
Derek There's no art to read the mind's construction in the face,
  Shakespeare said.
Brian You can say that again. Mother's been no better than she
  ought. All that Vitia Lampada nonsense!
Ray Most people put on an act at some time. Mrs Marsh is
  certainly putting on one now.

Amy enters

Any luck?
Amy No. I didn't expect any. It was only a formality. Stella said

she'd keep an eye on Mrs Marsh, so there's little more I can do.
Derek Will you release her?
Ray Looks like I'll have to.
Amy She had been out. The sole of one of her slippers was damp.
Ray I knew it. But where the devil did she put the necklace?
Derek Could it be in Stella's bedroom?
Ray She hadn't time to get outside, into the lounge and out again, and then upstairs during the time of your—resuscitation.

Derek eyes Ray suspiciously, and wipes his mouth

She may just have made it back into the hall, and led us to believe that she'd come downstairs. We weren't paying much attention at the time.
Derek (*sourly*) No. There was a case of attempted patricide.
Ray (*mechanically taking out his pipe*) I didn't expect tears. Out of character, that. Her sort don't.
Brian She was upset.
Ray I'm a bit sceptical about blinding tears, till I know who's being blinded.
Amy There's chivalry for you.
Derek I thought that Stella behaved rather well. The way she wiped Romaine's eyes and comforted her. Quite touching.
Ray I've been thinking about that—and the gold watch they said they'd been accused of taking. (*He takes the tobacco-pouch from the table*)
Derek What the devil are you getting at?
Ray Old school ties. Loyalties. (*He abstractedly presses tobacco into the bowl of his pipe. Almost unaware of what he is doing*)
Derek You're mad! Stella would never consent to anything like that. Besides, she's been searched.
Ray If we could find out where that necklace is, we'd have a pretty good idea who took it.

Derek and Brian are watching him, fascinated

I'm going to have one last try. It's only a theory, but I think I've got it. (*He puts the pipe in his mouth not yet aware that something is dangling from the bowl*)
Brian It—it's a bit stringy, isn't it?

Stella and Romaine appear unnoticed at the bottom of the stairs.

Stella claps her hand to her mouth, and they fall into each other's arms in silent mirth

Ray What?
Brian The tobacco.
Ray (*realising*) What the hell——!
Romaine (*coming forward, apparently serious*) Is that the necklace, Inspector? What will the police get up to next?
Ray (*furious*) Who the devil put that in my tobacco-pouch?
Romaine You surely don't think that either of us did it?
Ray (*heavily sarcastic*) Perish the thought! I blame the tobacco companies. They'll stick at nothing to promote their products. I came here to investigate a serious crime, not to play damned silly games with middle-aged schoolgirls.
Stella That's not a very nice thing for a police officer to say.
Ray You may have prevented me from bringing a charge, but you haven't prevented me speaking my mind.
Derek Very strong, old school ties, Ray. You said so yourself.
Ray Yes. It was a gross dereliction of duty on somebody's part that they weren't hung by them—from the parallel bars.
Stella I think you'd better go.
Ray Don't worry! We're going. Come on, Amy—before you have to report a murder.

He strides to the door in high dudgeon. Amy starts to follow

Derek I wonder if we shall meet again.
Stella That would be wasting police time.
Ray My God!

Ray goes out

Amy (*laughing*) I'm afraid you'll have to turn to crime.
Derek Issue a warning to all banks. I could be dangerous.

Amy follows Ray out

Brian I'd have been better off with the Mafia. I'm going to bed.
Derek Me, too. Bit of a headache, selling houses. If you do a deal, Stella, insist on cash.

Derek and Brian go upstairs

Romaine I'd rather forgotten about that. I suppose you wouldn't consider——?

Stella No, I would not, you devil. I want you out. I've paid my debt to you to-night, and I don't want to see you again—ever. I've stopped taking gold watches.
Romaine I saved you from being expelled.
Stella And I've saved you from being imprisoned. We're quits, so get out.
Romaine A pity. (*She picks the necklace from the table*) It's a nice necklace.
Stella Hands off!
Romaine We might even have slept together again.
Stella (*firmly*) Good-bye, Romaine!
Romaine Good-bye, Stella! And thank you!

She kisses Stella gently on the cheek, and goes out

Stella stands in thought for a few seconds, then picks up the necklace

Derek appears at the bottom of the stairs

Derek Have you been into my wallet, Stella?
Stella No. Why?
Derek That two hundred and fifty quid I drew out for the car. It's gone.
Stella My God! She never misses a trick.

Derek moves towards the hall

What are you going to do?
Derek Phone the local police, of course.
Stella Don't! Let her go.
Derek Why, for God's sake?
Stella Because of—what she may think.

Derek stands undecided, baffled by the complexity of the feminine mind, as——

the Curtain *falls*

FURNITURE AND PROPERTY LIST

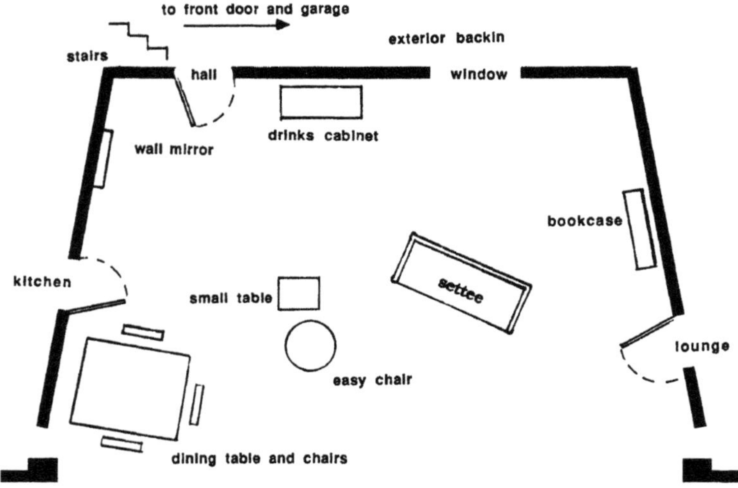

On stage: Curtains
Carpet
Dining table and chairs
Settee
Easy chair
Bookcase
Drinks cabinet. *In it:* glasses, whisky, Bacardi, gin, mixers etc.
Table lamp
Small table
Wall mirror
Large ornamental jar

Off stage: Nightdress, slippers, dressing-gown. *In pocket:* large handkerchief **(Romaine)**
Nightdress, down and feathers **(Stella)**
Tray with coffee and sandwiches, pyjamas, dustpan and brush **(Derek)**

Pyjamas **(Brian)**
Stage blood **(Ray)**

Personal: **Romaine:** coat, handbag
Ray: coat, pipe, tobacco pouch. *In it:* necklace. Keys, torch, ID
card
Derek: keys

LIGHTING PLOT

Practical fittings required: table lamp

Interior. The same scene throughout

To open: Evening: subdued interior lighting. Table lamp on

Cue 1   **Stella** switches on the lights   (Page 1)
Bring up lights in living-room and hall/staircase area

Cue 2   **Ray** switches off the main lights and the table lamp   (Page 15)
Semi-darkness

Cue 3   **Ray** settles down on the settee   (Page 15)
Semi-darkness dims to Black-out. Slowly bring up bluish moonlight

Cue 4   **Brian** switches on the lights   (Page 16)
Bring up lights in living-room and hall/staircase area

EFFECTS PLOT